Love

A Book of Quotations

We conceal it from ourselves in vain – we must always love something. In those matters seemingly removed from love, the feeling is secretly to be found, and man cannot possibly live for a moment without it.

Blaise Pascal

Love, free as air at sight of human ties,
Spreads his light wings, and in a moment flies.
Alexander Pope

If so many men, so many minds,
certainly so many hearts, so many kinds of love.

Leo Tolstoy

If I speak in the tongues of men and of angels, but have
not love, I am only a resounding gong or a clanging cymbal.
If I have the gift of prophecy and can fathom all mysteries and
all knowledge, and if I have a faith that can move mountains,
but have not love, I am nothing.
If I give all I possess to the poor and surrender my body
to the flames, but have not love, I gain nothing.
Love is patient, love is kind.
It does not envy, it does not boast, it is not proud.

It is not rude, it is not self-seeking, it is not easily angered,
it keeps no record of wrongs.
Love does not delight in evil but rejoices with the truth.
It always protects, always trusts, always hopes,
always perseveres.
Love never fails. . . .
And now these three remain: faith, hope and love.
But the greatest of these is love.

1 Corinthians 13 NIV

We are all born for love;
it is the principle of existence and its only end.
Benjamin Disraeli

To love and be loved is to feel the sun
from both sides.

David Viscott

Oh, innocent victims of Cupid,
Remember this terse little verse;
To let a fool kiss you is stupid,
To let a kiss fool you is worse.

E Y Harburg

To leave is to die a little;
It is to die to what one loves.
One leaves behind a little of oneself
At any hour, any place.
Edmond Haraucourt

Love is an act of endless forgiveness,
a tender look which becomes a habit.

Peter Ustinov

Sometimes when one person is missing,
the whole world seems depopulated.

Lamartine

If a thing loves, it is infinite.
William Blake

In dreams and in love there are no impossibilities.

Janos Arany

Love and work are the cornerstones of our humanness.

Sigmund Freud

Love me or hate me, but spare me your indifference.

Libbie Fudim

There is a courtesy of the heart; it is allied to love.
From it springs the purest courtesy in
the outward behaviour.

Johann Wolfgang von Goethe

We look forward to the time when the power to love
will replace the love of power. Then will our world
know the blessings of peace.

William Gladstone

Love is, above all, the gift of oneself.

Jean Anouilh

A compliment is like a kiss through a veil.

Victor Hugo

Man must evolve for all human conflict a method
which rejects revenge, aggression and retaliation.
The foundation of such a method is love.

Martin Luther King, Jr.

Love, I find, is like singing. Everybody can do enough to satisfy themselves, though it may not impress the neighbours as being very much.

Zora Neale Hurston

To love someone deeply gives you strength.
Being loved by someone deeply gives you courage.

Lao Tzu

Love is the delusion that one man or woman
differs from another.

H L Mencken

Do you want me to tell you something really subversive?
Love is everything it's cracked up to be.
That's why people are so cynical about it. . . .
It really is worth fighting for, being brave for,
risking everything for.
And the trouble is, if you don't risk anything,
you risk even more.

Erica Jong

Love is what we are born with. Fear is what we learn.
The spiritual journey is the unlearning of fear and prejudices
and the acceptance of love back in our hearts.
Love is the essential reality and our purpose on earth.
To be consciously aware of it, to experience love in ourselves
and others, is the meaning of life. Meaning does not lie
in things. Meaning lies in us.

Marianne Williamson

Neither a lofty degree of intelligence nor imagination
nor both together go to the making of genius.
Love, love, love, that is the soul of genius.

Wolfgang Amadeus Mozart

Accept the things to which fate binds you,
and love the people with whom fate brings you together,
but do so with all your heart.

Marcus Aurelius

'Love is the only thing that we can carry with us
when we go, and it makes the end so easy.'
from Good Wives by Louisa May Alcott

A man in love is incomplete until he is married.
Then he's finished.

Zsa Zsa Gabor

To love another person is to help them love God.

Søren Kierkegaard

Love is a hole in the heart.

Ben Hecht

The love of liberty is the love of others.
The love of power is the love of ourselves.

William Hazlit

Age does not protect you from love.
But love, to some extent, protects you from age.
Jeanne Moreau

I know for me the subject of how to be in
a relationship is precious and complicated and challenging.
It wouldn't be right to make it look too easy.

Helen Hunt

Lots of people are willing to die for the person they love, which is a pity, for it is a much grander thing to live for that person.

Jason Hurst

To hide the key to your heart is to risk forgetting where you placed it.

Timothy P Childers

Love, all alike, no season knows, nor clime,
Nor hours, age, months, which are the rags of time.
John Donne

Absence from whom we love is worse than death,
and frustrates hope severer than despair.
William Cowper

Intimacy, n. A relation into which fools are providentially drawn for their mutual destruction.

Ambrose Bierce

There is hardly any, any enterprise, which is
started out with such tremendous hopes and expectations,
and yet which fails so regularly, as love.
Erich Fromm

Love is the word used to label the sexual excitement
of the young, the habituation of the middle-aged,
and the mutual dependence of the old.

John Ciardi

There is only one sort of love,
but there are a thousand copies.
François de la Rochefoucauld

A coward is incapable of exhibiting love;
it is the prerogative of the brave.
Mahatma Gandhi

We are shaped and fashioned by what we love.

Johann Wolfgang von Goethe

Love is a great beautifier.
Louisa May Alcott

You will find as you look back upon your life
that the moments when you have really lived
are the moments when you have done things
in the spirit of love.

Henry Drummond

Love, with very young people, is a heartless
business. We drink at that age from thirst,
or to get drunk; it is only later in life that we occupy
ourselves with the individuality of our wine.

Isak Dinesen

Love is union with somebody, or something, outside oneself, under the condition of retaining the separateness and integrity of one's own self.

Erich Fromm

W e don't love qualities, we love persons;
sometimes by reason of their defects as well
as of their qualities.

Jacques Maritain

We are not the same persons this year as last;
nor are those we love. It is a happy chance if we,
changing, continue to love a changed person.

W Somerset Maugham

Love is the principal means of escape from
the loneliness which afflicts most men and women
throughout the greater part of their lives.

Bertrand Russell

For hatred does not cease by hatred at any time:
hatred ceases by love – this is the eternal law.

Pali Canon

If you're in a relationship and you want to
make it work, you have to be a little selfless at times.
Montel Williams

Love is not enough. It must be the foundation,
the cornerstone – but not the complete structure.
It is much too pliable, too yielding.

Bette Davis

Friendship is a disinterested commerce
between equals; love, an abject intercourse between
tyrants and slaves.

Oliver Goldsmith

No one perfectly loves God who does not perfectly
love some of his creatures.

Marguerite de Valois

Paradise was made for tender hearts;
hell, for loveless hearts.

Voltaire

Let love be your greatest aim.

1 Corinthians 14:1

For an instant, love can transform the world.

Author Unidentified

Among those whom I like or admire, I can find
no common denominator, but among those whom I love,
I can: all of them make me laugh.

W H Auden

All love is sweet,
Given or returned. Common as light is love,
And its familiar voice wearies not ever.

Shelley

When you're in a relationship, you're always
surrounded by a ring of circumstances . . .
joined together by a wedding ring, or in a boxing ring.

Bob Seger

When women love us, they forgive us everything,
even our crimes; when they do not love us,
they give us credit for nothing, not even our virtues.

Honore de Balzac

Some emotions don't make a lot of noise.
It's hard to hear pride. Caring is real faint –
like a heartbeat. And pure love – why, some days
it's so quiet, you don't even know it's there.
Erma Bombeck

The truth is that there is only one terminal dignity –
love. And the story of love is not important – what is
important is that one is capable of love. It is perhaps
the only glimpse we are permitted of eternity.

Helen Hayes

Anyone can hate. It costs to love.

John Williamson

Love tells us many things that are not so.

Ukranian Proverb

Love is the triumph of imagination over intelligence.

H L Mencken

Hell is a place, a time, a consciousness, Richard,
in which there is no love.

Richard Bach

Who, being loved, is poor?

Oscar Wilde

Love conquers all.

Virgil

Love seems the swiftest, but it is the slowest
of growths. No man or woman really knows
what perfect love is until they have been married
a quarter of a century.

Mark Twain

Who seeks for Heaven alone to save his soul
May keep the path, but will not reach the goal;
While he who walks in love may wander far,
Yet God will bring him where the blessed are.

Henry Van Dyke

Love does not dominate; it cultivates.

Johann Wolfgang von Goethe

Assumptions are the termites of relationships.

Henry Winkler

The opposite of love, I have found, is not hate,
but indifference.
Elie Weisel

Never forget that the most powerful force
on earth is love.

Nelson Rockefeller

To write a good love letter, you ought to begin without knowing what you mean to say, and to finish without knowing what you have written.

Jean Jacques Rousseau

When we love something it is of value to us,
and when something is of value to us we spend time
with it, time enjoying it and time taking care of it.

M Scott Peck

If we discovered that we only had five minutes left to say all that we wanted to say, every telephone booth would be occupied by people calling other people to stammer that they loved them.

Christopher Morley

Love many things, for therein lies the true strength,
and whosoever loves much performs much,
and can accomplish much, and what is done in love
is well done.

Vincent Van Gogh

It is easy to love the people far away.
It is not always easy to love those close to us.
It is easier to give a cup of rice to relieve hunger
than to relieve the loneliness and pain of someone
unloved in our own home. Bring love into your home
for this is where our love for each other must start.

Mother Teresa

Some truths between husband and wife must be
spoken, but let them be spoken with sweetness.
Wounded vanity is fatal to love. It makes one hate
the person who inflicted the wound.
In married conversation, as in surgery,
the knife must be used with care.

Andre Maurois

A successful marriage requires falling in love
many times, always with the same person.
Mignon McLaughlin

The happiness of married life depends upon making small sacrifices with readiness and cheerfulness.

John Seldon

Love all, trust a few;
Do wrong to none.
William Shakespeare, All's Well That Ends Well

Unable are the Loved to die
For Love is Immortality.
Emily Dickinson

The love we give away is the only love we keep.

Elbert Hubbard

You can't buy love, but you can pay heavily for it.

Henny Youngman

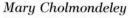

Every day I live I am more convinced
that the waste of life lies in the love we have not given,
the powers we have not used, the selfish prudence
that will risk nothing and which, shirking pain,
misses happiness as well.

Mary Cholmondeley

Happiness comes more from loving
than being loved; and often when our affection
seems wounded it is is only our vanity bleeding.
To love, and to be hurt often, and to love again –
this is the brave and happy life.

J E Buchrose

In delay there lies no plenty;
Then come kiss me, sweet and twenty,
Youth's a stuff will not endure.
William Shakespeare

An act of love that fails is just as much a part
of the divine life as an act of love that succeeds,
for love is measured by fullness, not by reception.

Harold Loukes

The perfect love affair is one which is conducted
entirely by post.

George Bernard Shaw

Love is an emotion experienced by the many
and enjoyed by the few.
George Jean Nathan

Love one another and you will be happy.
It's as simple and as difficult as that.
Michael Leunig

People need loving the most
when they deserve it the least.

John Harrigan

It is better to be hated for what you are
than to be loved for what you are not.
Andre Gide

In literature as in love, we are astonished
at what is chosen by others.

André Maurois

An ounce of love is worth a pound of knowledge.

John Wesley

Love is shown in your deeds, not in your words.

Fr. Jerome Cummings

Love looks through a telescope;
envy, through a microscope.

Josh Billings

I don't want to live.
I want to love first, and live incidentally.
Zelda Fitzgerald

Love does not consist in gazing at each other,
but in looking together in the same direction.

Saint-Exupéry

Keep love in your heart. A life without it
is like a sunless garden when the flowers are dead.

Oscar Wilde

The fickleness of the women I love
is only equalled by the infernal consistency
of the women who love me.

George Bernard Shaw

It is a curious thought, but it is only when
you see people looking ridiculous that you realise
just how much you love them.

Agatha Christie

If you have love you will do all things well.

Thomas Merton

More than kisses, letters mingle souls.

John Donne

Love is the great miracle cure.
Loving ourselves works miracles in our lives.
Louise Hay

There is only one path to Heaven.
On Earth, we call it Love.

Karen Goldman

Looking back, I have this to regret, that too often
when I loved, I did not say so.

David Grayson

If you find it in your heart to care for somebody else,
you will have succeeded.

Maya Angelou

Honour the ocean of love.

George de Benneville

If you first don't succeed in love, try a little ardour.

Anon

I want to do with you
What spring does
With the cherry trees.
Pablo Neruda

. . . She thinks me young,
Although she knows my days are past the best.
William Shakespeare

Love is like quicksilver in the hand. Leave the fingers open and it stays. Clutch it, and it darts away.

Dorothy Parker

What is lovely never dies,
But passes into other loveliness.
Thomas Bailey

To love is to receive a glimpse of heaven.

Karen Sunde

We can only learn to love by loving.

Iris Murdoch

If the soul is to know itself it must look into a soul.

George Seferis

Love is always in the mood of believing in miracles.

John Cowper Powys

Those that go searching for love only
make manifest their own lovelessness,
and the loveless never find love, only the loving
find love, and they never have to seek for it.

D H Lawrence

When I look on you a moment, then I can speak no more,
but my tongue falls silent, and at once a delicate flame
courses beneath my skin, and with my eyes I see nothing,
and my ears hum, and dampness bathes me
and a trembling seizes me all over . . .

Sappho

It is with our passions as with fire and water, they are good servants, but bad masters.

Roger L'Estrange

Who loves not wine, women or song
Remains a fool his whole life long.

Martin Luther

Where there is love there is no sense either.

Dostoevsky

Music, moody food of us that trade in love.
William Shakespeare: Antony and Cleopatra

When one loves somebody, everything is clear –
where to go, what to do – it all takes care of itself
and one doesn't have to ask anybody about anything.
Maxim Gorky

If he said quit drinking martinis, but I kept on drinking them and next morning I couldn't get out of bed, he wouldn't tell me he told me so.

Judith Viorst

Y ou must love all that God has created, both his entire world
and each single tiny sand grain of it. Love each tiny leaf,
each beam of sunshine. You must love the animals,
love every plant. If you love all things, you will also attain
the divine mystery that is in all things. For then the ability
to perceive the truth will grow every day, and your mind
will open itself to an all-embracing love.

Fyodor Dostoyevsky

Terrified again of not loving,
of loving and not loving you,
of being loved and not by you.
If you do not love me
I shall not be loved,
if I do not love you
I shall not love

Samuel Beckett: Cascando

Spread love everywhere you go . . . let no one
ever come to you without leaving better and happier.
Be the living expression of God's kindness; kindness
in your face, kindness in your eyes, kindness in
your smile, kindness in your warm greeting.

Mother Teresa

A difficult achievement for true lovers
Is to lie mute,
Without embrace or kiss,
Without a rustle or a smothered sigh,
Basking in each other's glory.

Robert Graves

No one has ever loved anyone the way
everyone wants to be loved.
Mignon McLaughlin

It needs no dictionary of quotations to remind me
that eyes are the windows of the soul.

Max Beerbohm

Kissing power is stronger than will power . . .
Abigail Van Buren

Life is short. Be swift to love!
Make haste to be kind!
Henri F Amiel

Treasure the love you receive above all.
It will survive long after your gold and good health
have vanished.
Og Mandino

One word
Frees us of all the weight and pain of life:
That word is love.

Sophocles

Love that is hoarded moulds at last
Until we know some day
The only thing we ever have
Is what we give away.

Louis Ginsberg